Create and Share | Thinking Digitally

Staying Safe Online

By Adrienne Matteson

Published in the United States of America by:

CHERRY LAKE PRESS

2395 South Huron Parkway, Suite 200, Ann Arbor, Michigan
www.cherrylakepublishing.com

Series Adviser: Kristin Fontichiaro
Reading Adviser: Marla Conn, MS, Ed., Literacy specialist, Read-Ability, Inc.
Book Designer: Felicia Macheske
Character Illustrator: Rachael McLean

Photo Credits: © DGLimages/Shutterstock.com, 7; © Rob Marmion/Shutterstock.com, 13; © fizkes/Shutterstock.com, 17;
© Oksana Kuzmina/Shutterstock.com, 19; © Syda Productions/Shutterstock.com, 21

Graphics Throughout: © the simple surface/Shutterstock.com; © Diana Rich/Shutterstock.com; © lemony/Shutterstock.com;
© CojoMoxon/Shutterstock.com; © IreneArt/Shutterstock.com; © Artefficient/Shutterstock.com; © Marie Nimrichterova/Shutterstock.
com; © Svetolk/Shutterstock.com; © EV-DA/Shutterstock.com; © briddy/Shutterstock.com; © Mix3r/Shutterstock.com

Library of Congress Cataloging-in-Publication Data

Names: Matteson, Adrienne, author. | McLean, Rachael, illustrator.
Title: Staying safe online / by Adrienne Matteson ; illustrated by Rachael McLean.
Description: Ann Arbor, Michigan : Cherry Lake Publishing, 2020. | Series:
Create and share : thinking digitally | Includes index. | Audience:
Grades 2-3.
Identifiers: LCCN 2019033473 (print) | LCCN 2019033474 (ebook) |
ISBN 9781534159105 (hardcover) | ISBN 9781534161405 (paperback) |
ISBN 9781534160255 (pdf) | ISBN 9781534162556 (ebook)
Subjects: LCSH: Internet—Safety measures—Juvenile literature.
Classification: LCC HV6773 .M383 2020 (print) | LCC HV6773 (ebook) | DDC
025.042028/9—dc23
LC record available at https://lccn.loc.gov/2019033473
LC ebook record available at https://lccn.loc.gov/2019033474

Cherry Lake Publishing would like to acknowledge the work of the Partnership for 21st Century Learning, a Network of Battelle
for Kids. Please visit *www.battelleforkids.org/networks/p21* for more information.

Printed in the United States of America
Corporate Graphics

CHERRY LAKE PRESS

Table of
CONTENTS

CHAPTER ONE

Safety Rules

How do you stay safe? Are there places you know not to go? People you don't talk to? Rules you follow? You probably stay safe by doing all of these things. Safety rules help to keep you from getting hurt or lost. Almost anywhere you go, there are safety rules for you to follow. Some rules, like "Don't run" and "Don't talk to strangers," will help you stay safe in almost all situations. Special safety rules for school and playgrounds protect you from dangers **unique** to those places. Even at home, you have rules to follow.

The internet is another place with unique dangers. But there are **commonsense** rules that will help you stay safe while you are **online**.

How do you know what these rules are? You can start by asking your teacher. Your school already has a list of internet safety rules. It's called an Acceptable Use Policy, or AUP. Reading and signing an AUP usually means you promise:

- To be respectful of other kids and their work
- Not to use school technology to look up dangerous or **inappropriate** websites
- Not to use school technology to break the law

Following AUP rules is a great way to stay safe and be respectful to others when you are online.

Rules keep you safe at school.

Online vs. Offline Safety Rules

How are online safety rules like the safety rules you follow in your home and at school?

On a piece of paper, make a Venn diagram. A Venn diagram consists of two big circles that overlap in the middle. Title one circle "Online" and the other circle "Real World." Write all of the safety rules you can think of for each side. In the middle, write safety rules that you follow both in the real world and online. What are some safety rules that are true online and in the real world? What are some safety rules that you only need to think about when you are online? Ask your teacher and parents to help you make your list.

Some safety rules are the same everywhere.

RULES

Online

Real World

Be respectful of other people online.

CHAPTER TWO

Privacy and Safety

The internet is a wide-open place. It's full of people you don't know who can see the things you post online. When you meet a stranger in real life, you don't tell that person everything about yourself. You should follow the same rules online. Keep information about you and the people you care about **private**. This means that only you and the people you trust the most know that information. Don't tell who you are or where you are with people you don't know.

WHO You Are

Keep your **identity** private online by never using your real or full name. Keep your friends and family safe too by following these same rules. Don't post a picture or video of anyone without asking for their permission. That includes family members and friends. Some people don't want pictures of themselves on the internet.

Keep your identity secret.

TOP SECRET

WHERE You Are

Never tell someone online where you live, go to school, or spend your time. Do your parents allow you to use **social media**, like Instagram? If so, keep posts and stories about where you are private. This is especially true if you're posting in **real time**. Or you can always wait to post your photos and videos from vacation or school trips until after you return home.

Some social media websites and **apps** are set to include your location when you post. You might need to change the **privacy settings** on that app to keep your location private. Ask an adult to help you look at these settings and change them if necessary. It's a good idea to check the privacy settings for social media a few times a year.

Create Safe Passwords

Having strong passwords will help keep your information private online. It's easy to have the same password for everything. But that's not the safest idea. Plan to have a different password for every **account** you make online. The best passwords are *easy* for you to remember, but *hard* for other people to guess.

A good password:

- Has more than eight letters and numbers
- Is a mix of letters (capital and lowercase), numbers, and special **characters** (like $ and #)
- Does not include anything about you that someone can guess—like your birthday, name, pet's name, or address

Think of a sentence or a line from a song you love. Then use only the first letter from every word. For example, "Blue and sea green are my favorite colors" becomes "basgamfc." Now replace a few letters with numbers and capital letters: "Ba$GaMfC."

Your turn! On a piece of paper, use these rules to brainstorm three or four safe passwords.

PASSWORD

Safe passwords are hard for other people to guess.

CHAPTER THREE

Safety Zones

The best way to find safe places on the internet is to follow the advice of people you know and trust. At school, your teacher and media specialist can guide you to websites that are safe and full of good information. If your school library has a website, check there to find good sites.

Your library might even **subscribe** to kid-friendly **databases**, like PebbleGo or Britannica Kids. These are safe and help make learning fun for kids!

Ask your media specialist for help.

Another good place to look for safe sites is your public library website. Most have a list of databases and websites just for kids. Have your library card ready in case you need it to log in.

Social websites made for school use are also safe spaces. These include Google Classroom, Code.org, Scratch, and Seesaw.

Databases have a lot of information.

Set SafeSearch on Google

You can set up Google on your home computer to only search for safe websites. Google has a setting called SafeSearch. It can be turned on and off. Or you can lock it in your settings, so that SafeSearch is always turned on. You will need a parent to log in to their Google account.

Instructions:

1. Go to Google.com.
2. Look for the word "Settings" at the very bottom of the page. Click on it.
3. A menu will pop up. Click on the top choice in the menu that says "Search Settings."
4. At the top of this page, click the box that says "Turn on SafeSearch." Next to that is the option to "Lock SafeSearch." Your parent will need to use their password to lock SafeSearch. It will always be turned on until your parent turns it off.

You can also use kid-friendly **search engines**, like Kiddle or KidRex. Ask your school or local librarian for more information!

CHAPTER FOUR

Safe and Alert!

There will be times when you need to use websites that are not in a safe database or made for kids to use. When that happens, stay aware and tell a grown-up when something isn't right.

Be on the lookout for websites that don't seem trustworthy. Avoid ones that use words and pictures that make you uncomfortable. Don't be fooled by sites with lots of advertisements or that promise rewards if you "Click Here!" Clicking there could harm your computer or take you to an unsafe website.

Tell an adult when you see something that is wrong.

The internet isn't just a place to find information. For a lot of people, it is where they talk to friends, play games, and share their thoughts, pictures, and videos. Talk to your parents about how you want to use the internet. Always ask permission before you create an account on a social media or gaming site. Follow the rules in chapter 2 to keep your information safe and private. And if another user says or posts something that makes you uncomfortable or upset, tell a trusted adult. All social media and gaming sites have a way to report users who are not safe and respectful.

Internet filters block adult websites at school.

Have you ever clicked on a link at school only to get a message that says that website is "blocked?" At school, they use **filters** to keep students from visiting dangerous or inappropriate websites. Most filters use keywords to decide what websites are blocked. Some filters are set to block all websites of a certain kind, like gaming or shopping websites. Filters help keep you safe online when you are at school.

Be Alert!

It can be difficult to know what to look for when you are watching for things that seem wrong online. On a piece of paper, brainstorm the warning signs that would make you tell an adult or leave a website. Circle a few that seem the most important to you. Make a poster to help you remember what to look out for on the internet. Put your poster where you'll see it when you are on the computer.

Here are some examples of warning signs:

- Messages that pop up on a website that say things like "CLEAN NOW. YOUR COMPUTER IS AT RISK!"
- Websites with more ads than text
- Receiving an email from a stranger that has a link
- There isn't any contact information at the website

Share what you've learned with friends and family. Maybe make a poster for them too!

Always ask before you create an account.

GLOSSARY

account (uh-KOUNT) a requirement some websites have where they ask for your personal information before allowing you into the site; it usually requires a username and password

apps (APPZ) computer programs, usually on a smartphone or tablet

characters (KAR-ik-turz) numbers, letters, or special symbols

commonsense (KAH-muhn-sens) showing good judgment

databases (DAY-tuh-base-iz) parts of the internet that hold a lot of information and are accessed at school or with a login

filters (FIL-turz) computer programs that control what kinds of websites are blocked and not blocked at a school or library

identity (eye-DEN-tih-tee) the information that makes up who you are on the internet

inappropriate (in-uh-PROH-pree-it) not right or proper for the situation, time, or place

online (AWN-line) connected to the internet

privacy settings (PRYE-vuh-see SET-ingz) controls on a social media account that can limit how much other users can learn about you

private (PRYE-vit) belonging to only one person or group of people and not shared with anyone else

real time (REEL TIME) actual time during which something takes place

search engines (SURCH EN-jinz) software that looks online for information it thinks matches your keywords and past history

social media (SOH-shuhl MEE-dee-uh) a website or app designed for talking and sharing with other people

subscribe (suhb-SKRIBE) to pay money regularly for a product or service

unique (yoo-NEEK) different from everything else

BOOK

Bedford, David. *Once Upon a Time… Online: Happily Ever After Is Only a Click Away!* Bath, England: Parragon Inc. 2016.

WEBSITES

Common Sense Education—Ready to Play Digital Passport?
https://www.commonsense.org/education/digital-passport
Learn more about how to safely navigate the internet.

Junior SafeSearch
https://www.juniorsafesearch.com
Discover more online using this kid-friendly search engine that blocks and filters potentially harmful sites and images.

Kiddle
www.kiddle.co
Navigate and search the internet safely with this search engine designed with kids in mind.

INDEX

About the AUTHOR

Adrienne Matteson is a middle school librarian in Atlanta, Georgia. When she is not teaching her students to be good digital citizens, she is knitting, singing, serving the community, and doing her best to make a positive footprint of her own.